Thrift Store Diva

Spending Pennies and Looking Like a Million Dollars

Helen J. Pearson

Printed and Bound in the United States of America
Published and Distributed by:
Professional Publishing House
1425 W. Manchester Ave. Ste. B
Los Angeles, CA 90047
(323) 750-3592
drrosie@aol.com
www.professionalpublishinghouse.com

Cover layout: Richard Ike
Formatting: Professional Publishing House
First printing, February 2012
ISBN: 978-0-9834444-4-2

DEDICATION

This book is dedicated to every woman who loves style, fashion and elegance, but has a low budget due to the economy. It shows you how to shop with pennies, and how to look like a million dollars.

ACKNOWLEDGMENTS

Several individuals played central roles in shaping the ideas and realization of this completed work.

First, my deepest gratitude goes to my Lord and Savior, Jesus Christ, who gave me the ability to be creative. I thank you Lord for revealing Your-self to me, and for leading, guiding, and ordering my steps into the thrift stores.

My special thanks to the precious Holy Spirit which gave me the insight, knowledge, and wisdom that enabled me to write this book about "Thrifting."

I give special credit and thanks to my BFF, Louise Burnett, who inspired and encouraged me to write this book, and whose ideas became a reality when we both obeyed the Holy Spirit. She planted the seed of the idea and watered it with prayer. She also named the title of this book, *Thrift Store Diva.* To her, I am especially grateful.

To my wonderful sons, Patrick and Garrick Huff, who also inspired and encouraged me. Patrick penned the "Book Endorsement," and Garrick penned "About the Author."

Their contributions are very much appreciated, and I thank them from the bottom of my heart.

To my dear sister, Doris Matthews, thanks for being my beautiful sister and model. You are the greatest. Your unconditional love and support have made me into the woman I am today. Thanks a million.

Special thanks to my longtime friend, Barbara Ryals, who also has been an inspiration to me and an encourager. She, too, is my BFF. We have been friends for over sixty-five years, and she has always believed in me. I am eternally grateful.

I give a special thank you and my appreciation to my photographer, Lisa Mosely, who took these lovely pictures.

May God bless each of you.

CONTENTS

From a Friend's Perspective, 9

About the Author, 11

The Thrift Store Diva, 13

Foreword, 15

Introduction, 17

CHAPTER 1

*How to Shop with Pennies and Look Like a
Million Dollars*, 19

CHAPTER 2

A Born "Diva," 24

CHAPTER 3

Thrifting Can Be Fun—And The Rules for Shopping, 29

CHAPTER 4

Seven Reasons to Be a Thrifter, 34

CHAPTER 5

What's Color Got To Do With It?, 37

CHAPTER 6

Let the Show Begin!!!!!!, 40

Conclusion, 71

From A Friend's Perspective

Helen Pearson is one of the sharpest dressers I know. When I learned she purchased most of her clothes, shoes and accessories from the thrift store, and was not ashamed to let people know it, I told her that there are people that need to know they could look like a million dollars for only pennies, too. I encouraged her to write this book to share her knowledge about thrift store shopping and finding countless treasures. As I was reflecting on what a gift she has, the name of the book came to me—*Thrift Store Diva*. She is a diva, not with the negative connotations, but in a positive way. From her glamour to how she carries herself, a diva that knows how to do what she does so well.

—Louise Burnett

About the Author

Helen J. Pearson, a native of Memphis, Tennessee, is a woman of humble beginnings. Born the eldest of eight siblings, she learned the value of a dollar at a young age. Growing up in the south in the early 1940s, money was scarce for a family of ten. So Helen developed the ability of making her dollars stretch.

As the eldest sibling, Helen had to enter the workforce as a teenager. To help support her family, she worked as a maid. As a young lady, Helen was fascinated by fashion and envisioned one day becoming a fashionista. She had a rare eye for quality and learned to accessorize. This talent helped give her limited wardrobe a fresh, new look. Helen's love for fashion grew as she matured into an adult woman.

Several years have passed since that childhood dream, but the dream still lives on. Although Helen is now retired and a widow who has entered her "golden years," you would never know it by her appearance. Helen's sense of style and fashion flair is still very much in bloom and is as vibrant as ever.

Helen J. Pearson

The recent economic downturn has caused Helen to look for innovative ways to continue fulfilling her life-long passion for shopping. Now, living on a fixed income and a limited budget, Helen still possesses an unlimited desire to look her best. This would inspire her to write *Thrift Store Diva.*

A woman of faith, flair and favor, Helen J. Pearson spends her retirement years in faithful service at her local church, Glory Christian Fellowship International, where Alton Trimble is the Pastor. She still has a love for writing, and of course shopping. Her other published books are *From Sin To Glory* and *Poems of Inspiration.* She is the proud mother of two adult sons and two adult granddaughters. She currently resides in Long Beach, California.

— Garrick Huff,
Second Son of the Thrift Store Diva

THE THRIFT STORE DIVA

The Thrift Store Diva is a woman of style,
She will walk around all day, even for miles
Looking for bargains that will make her pop,
She loves shopping for clothes that are really hot.

The Thrift Store Diva is a woman of class,
Her body may not look like a Coca Cola bottle or an hourglass,
But the clothes she buys definitely compliment her figure,
Some women are envious, and the opposite sex digs her.

She loves dresses, suits, skirts, and trousers,
Pant suits, coats, sweaters, shirts and blouses,
Shoes, boots, purses, scarves, and hats,
Even costume jewelry, and that's a fact.

She looks for clothes that are a bargain, unbelievably priced,
Clothes on sale where the prices are slashed,
Clothes that are unique, even one of a kind,
To her, clothes that are different are a fantastic find.

She looks for clothes that are a perfect fit,
And of a good quality that makes you look chic,
Clothes that make you look stylish, and have people talking;
Clothes that will make a statement, ready for runway walking.

She is well groomed, sassy, and thrifty as can be,
She's tall, slender, with a friendly outgoing personality,
This attractive woman I am describing is unique you see,
The Thrift Store Diva is actually me!!

— Helen J. Pearson

FOREWORD

Over the years, I have learned that fashion comes and goes, but true style will last a lifetime. Clothing is an investment that should pay dividends, year in and year out. Clothing shapes your identity and, in many cases, your destiny as well.

Growing up with parents, who each conveyed exceptional style, helped me to appreciate the importance of style. Style is gained over time, much like wisdom. It is developed piece by piece, and many components are treasured due to the quality, design, and attention to detail in which it was made. Fine elements of clothing should appreciate over time, like fine art. What and how we wear clothing impacts every area of our lives—social, business, formal, and recreational.

My mother has mastered the art of impeccable style, grace, and significant elegance. Her God-given gift of putting together vibrant, head-turning, high quality, women wardrobe ensembles for pennies on the dollar, is simply remarkable. For years, family and friends have been blown away by her non-traditional shopping techniques, and the amazing prices attached to her acquisitions.

In today's recessionary times, our dollars need to stretch further, and this book will provide great insights of how, when, where, and why to shop like the Thrift Store Diva.

So if you are ready to take your attire, appearance, and level of self-confidence to a whole new level without breaking the bank, you must become a student of the Thrift Store Diva. She will prove that you can look like a million-dollar woman and save a fortune while doing so.

Patrick Huff,
Son of the Thrift Store Diva

INTRODUCTION

Thrift Store Diva is a visual book and a basic guide to thrift store shopping. It is an art often called thrifting, the act of shopping at a thrift store, flea market, or garage sale, usually with the intent of finding interesting items that may not be found at department stores at a cheap price. It actually means recycling of formerly owned items, finding new use and new love for vintage material goods, which was thrown out, and the thrill of discovering items that still have some life in them.

This book is a guide to help you understand the art of thrifting. It is written to give you tips on how to shop, where to shop, and when to shop. It will also give amazing tips on which thrift stores carry the best items. It advises you on the specials, half-off sale days, and what the color of the ticket means.

Thrift Store Diva has photographs of the many clothes, coats, shoes, bags, and jewelry I have purchased, how I have accessorized them, and how they are of very good quality and have designer labels. It also has a picture of my family room that I furnished from thrift store shopping.

As you read and look at the photographs, you will be amazed at the bold colors, and how elegant, stylish, and unique they are. You will see a fox fur stole and hat, different animal prints, exquisite church suits and dresses, evening attire, capes, vests, and the many pairs of shoes and bags to accent the outfits.

God gave the idea to my BFF (Best Friends Forever), and we put our talents together and came up with this beautiful book. I am the author and the purchaser of these clothes, and she is the business manager that does the displays and marketing. I know you will love this book, and it will help you look like a million dollars, while spending pennies, and you, too, can be a Thrift Store Diva.

CHAPTER 1

How to Shop with Pennies and Look Like a Million Dollars

With the sketchy economy, thrift store shopping is a practical way to save money, but even when the economic situation is in full bloom, it is a practical, reasonable, and easy way to stretch your dollars.

We live in inflationary times. As prices go up and up, you might find that shopping at thrift stores is the way to go.

Let's say you've decided to update your wardrobe and step out with a more glamorous or stylish look. Then you realize there's no way you will be able to pay $200.00 to $300.00 for a new outfit, not to mention accessories. So what is an innovative woman of fashion with a limited budget to do? The answer lies no further than your local thrift store.

Most thrift stores carry top quality, gently used clothing that can be bought for a fraction of their original cost. With so many of us on a strict budget due to the economy, it pays to revisit the option of pre-owned clothing.

If you haven't been to a Goodwill store, you will be pleasantly surprised by the quality. Even some items have the original price tags intact.

Now lots of people dislike thrift stores for a number of reasons. Often, some people feel they are "above" thrift stores, that they carry nothing but junk, and are dark, dirty, and depressing. While there are certainly some pretty dismal thrift stores out there, most are fairly clean and well organized, so I beg to differ.

Thrift shops are the best! Really! I frequent shops that are more like department stores. They get a lot of good-quality merchandise in, and most of the clothes I wear are from there, so I have no problem thrifting.

During this recession, I faced many challenges. Like many others, I struggled to pay my bills and make ends meet. In reality, my life was crumbling. I was getting depressed, fearful, doubtful, and pessimistic. If I didn't pull myself together, I would lose it.

My days and nights were filled with doom, gloom, loneliness and despair. I began to wonder if I would ever be able to do some of the things I loved to do. I admit, there were times I felt shattered, broken and helpless, and hope was no where to be found.

I didn't know what to do next, but I had to decide to look away from the terrible circumstances in my life and shift my attention to God. I knew only He could lift me out of my depression.

I learned in the hard times how to seek God and how to trust Him. He alone is my source. I learned to labor in prayer, study my Bible and worship. Once I confronted the hard realities of life, I fully appreciated how completely dependent I was on God. I clearly began to recognize that God was my only hope and source.

As I got my mind off me and on God, I sensed a ray of hope. God had given me a new lease on life, showing me how I could still enjoy what I loved to do and that was to shop. He showed me how to glorify Him and inspire others by the way I dressed.

Being a Christian woman, I am always aware of my appearance. Appearance is an unfading beauty and should be a compliment to God in every aspect of life. Maintaining a clean, neat, modest, and appropriate appearance is a responsibility. Suitable attire is essential for women who represent Christ. Style and beauty, however, need not be compromised. We can still be stylish with modesty and flair.

One of my hobbies is shopping. I love to shop and buy pretty things, but now I had no money. One day, while feeling lonely and depressed, I wandered into a thrift store just to browse and past some time, and I was amazed at what I saw. There were some awesome buys in that store.

Before I realized it, I had been in the thrift store about six hours. The whole time I was there, my mind was not on my dilemma, and time passed quickly. I began making it a ritual. Every day I would spend several hours in the thrift stores.

I would not be in a hurry. I took my time going through every rack. I discovered some fantastic items are tucked in between the junk.

It was like I was looking for hidden treasures and I found them. Some of the items were brand new, and still had the store price tags, and some had designer labels.

I soon realized this was good therapy, and it didn't cost me one dime.

The trips to the thrift stores were very therapeutic and I enjoyed being there. I started saving my little money and became a good steward of my time, money and talent.

I realized God had given me a gift, and that was to shop and put things together with very little money. You might say I was born to shop.

I shop thrift stores for myself, my family and my friends. The basic rule I follow is to look for quality/fit, and be willing to dig. Generally, I can run my eye down the racks and see which colors, patterns and materials catch my eye and have any chance of being right for my need.

I know some stores give to thrift stores when seasons change and they have not sold the items. Others give to thrift stores when items are returned, and have been worn or soiled with makeup.

Many people shop at high-end stores that have good return policies. They will buy an expensive outfit for a special occasion, wear it and return it to get their refund. They have no intention of keeping it. That is why it pays to take your time looking and not be in a rush. The good buys are there; you just have to search for them.

CHAPTER 2

A Born "Diva"

Ever since I was a little girl I have had a passion for glamour. Oh to be chic and glamorous! I had this dream where I would swoop into a room, head held high, stomach in, flawlessly attired, and not a hair out of place. Women would seethe with envy, and gentlemen would leap to their feet and offer a chair. I, like our First Lady, Michelle Obama, would smile regally, then sit down with knees together, and feet crossed at the ankles.

My gown is the latest fashion and it compliments every curve on my tall, slender body. When I speak, my voice is soft, but sure. I do not stammer or hesitate. I have the "it factor" and I know it. But then waking up and coming back to reality, I would say to myself, "One day I'm going to dress like that."

I have always had an eye for style and quality. I know when something looks cheap, and when it is something of value that will last and last. I learned very quickly how to accessorize and put outfits together. I learned that wearing a different blouse, sweater, or jacket could make a new outfit.

As the oldest of eight children and money was short, my parents could not afford to buy me new outfits often. That's when I learned the art of accessorizing. I also knew that by adding a pretty scarf or belt and the right jewelry, I could change an outfit from out-dated to outrageously beautiful.

Being the thrifty woman I am, and using the shopping gift God gave me, I learned to look for bargains. Before I started shopping in thrift stores, I shopped in basements of department stores, then I moved up to discount stores, and soon I shopped in the better department stores.

Bargain hunting has always been my hobby. I buy most things on sale: clothes, shoes, kitchen wares, books, you name it. The only time I purchase an item at regular price is when I really, really need a particular item and don't have time to hunt for it.

Remember, you don't have to sacrifice quality to get a great deal. Finding old and used treasures that cost next to nothing gives me thrill and excitement, so I decided to write this book to get connected with those fellow vintage and shabby chic lovers out there.

Being born in the era that I was, I loved things that matched, complimented, or accentuated the outfit. I will walk around all day looking for a specific color of shoes and bag that will match the outfit I am wearing.

I know what colors compliment my complexion, and I choose colors that make me pop. I love bright, bold, vibrant hues such as yellows, oranges, pinks, whites. Baby blues, navy blues, bright greens, reds, lavenders, purples, and fuchsias. I wear these colors in spring or summer. The darker colors such as blacks, browns, egg plants, cranberries, maroons, and grays are for fall and winter. I learned not to buy fads that would be out of style the next season, and I chose clothes that I could wear for years without looking outdated.

Mostly every day of my adult life, I get compliments on my appearance. Even when I don't think I'm looking great, people will come up to me and tell me how great I look, or ask where I bought the outfit. Most times I tell them, "from the thrift store," but they don't believe me.

I do not believe in half-stepping. My hair is nicely cut and styled. I am told that I am a stylish, well-groomed lady, and some say when they see me, they are looking at the whole package.

Sometimes, while driving down the street or stopped at a traffic light, horns will blow to get my attention. I think that I have done something wrong or the other driver is trying to warn me of some hazard or disaster, then I look at the other driver, and he or she points to my hair and compliments me on my style.

I have been asked by family and friends to shop for them when they want something special, and they have loved the items I purchased for them. I know designer labels and quality, so it's easy to pick out the good stuff from the junk.

I can find very expensive clothes for little or nothing. Now, I only shop at the thrift stores. I don't shop at the malls any more because I have found clothes from Neiman Marcus, Nordstrom, Macy's, and Bloomingdales all in the thrift stores.

Some of the designer labels I buy are: Ann Taylor, Ellen Tracy, Jones of New York, DKNY, Kasper, Anne Klein II, John Meyer, Bill Blass, Bicci, Larry Levine, Carole Little, Oleg Cassini, St. Anthony, Liz Claiborne, and St. John, just to name a few.

I have purchased jewelry, scarves, hats, fur coats, leather coats, wool coats with fur collars, a fox hat and stole, pant suits, skirt suits, skirts, blouses, sweaters, dresses, robes, lounge wear, and Dooney & Burke, Chanel, and Louis Vuitton purses. I also buy shoes from the thrift store—Nine West, St. John, Bellini, Bandolino, J. Renee', Liz Claiborne, Ann Marino, Enzo Angiolini—all brand new.

I have furnished my family room with furniture, pictures, wall plaques, lamps, wing back chairs, figurines, mirrors, coffee and end tables, plants, decorative throw pillows, TVs, and candle holders. I have purchased picture frames, candles, luggage, and appliances from the thrift stores. My favorite thrift stores are Goodwill, Salvation Army, AMVETS, and any other thrift store I find in the neighborhood. My closets are full, really overloaded with good buys. I have given away dozens of suits and dresses, and I still have more than I can ever wear. I have formal wear that looks like I paid hundreds of dollars for, and the most I have spent is $15.00. You name it, I have it. People tell me I look like a million dollars. They think I am wealthy, but I have only spent pennies.

I give God all the Glory for giving me the ideas and know-how to put an outfit together. You see God is the Creator, and I am made in His image; therefore, He has given me the ability to create magnificent outfits by simply knowing how to accessorize and knowing what colors compliment my skin tone.

CHAPTER 3

Thrifting Can Be Fun—And The Rules for Shopping

Thrifting is fun, and it's cheap. It's also a good deed, providing funds for various charities as well as keeping perfectly usable goods out of landfills and incinerators to provide a few more years of service.

If you're new to thrifting, here are a few pointers to help you make the most of a visit to a thrift store near you. I hope these tips will help you find those hidden treasures in your local thrift store.

KNOW WHERE TO LOOK, AND WHAT TO LOOK FOR

Not all thrift stores are created equal. Make a point to visit all the stores in your area, and take the time to search through them. You will soon find which stores carry the best merchandise and where to find it. Also, you must know quality. Feel the cloth things are made of. Is it a cheap weave? If you find a coat, is it cheaply made? Are the buckles made of plastic or metal? Know what makes a quality product, and what does not.

BE NICE

The people who work in thrift stores, as you can imagine, are not usually paid well, so be nice to them because it's the right thing to do. If you frequent a particular thrift store, you may even find that making yourself known and building relationships with the employees pays off with more than just good karma. If you have specific interests or needs, employees will often set aside things that might interest you or hold them behind the counter until you can get to the bank to pull money out.

KNOW THE SPECIALS

Many thrift stores run different kinds of specials for military and seniors citizens.

KNOW YOUR LOCAL STORE'S SALE DAYS

Many local Salvation Army stores have half-off Wednesdays and 40% off on Saturdays.

Try Things On

Always try things on. Just because it's a beautiful silk, Ann Taylor skirt doesn't mean you should buy it. If it doesn't fit well, it's a needless purchase. In some stores, the purchase is final. You cannot return it or exchange it.

Go With Cash

Leave your debit card and credit card at home. When you're armed with cash, you'll be more selective with your purchases. Also, some stores only take cash.

Go Regularly, And Go On Off-Hours

The first helps you acquire more goodies. The second is for sanity's sake. Seriously, if you don't go regularly, you are just asking to miss all the good loot. You can take this a step further and inquire about "restocking" day, as in, when do they do it? Then mark that day down in your little black book and make sure you go. Expert thrift shoppers go every day to their favorite stores. Be consistent and visit as many times a week as you can manage.

Shop Off-season

You'll find the best deals and have a better selection to pick through. Winter coats are plentiful, and purchased for pennies in August. I would imagine the same would go for vintage sun dresses during January.

Give some thought to a thrifting uniform. In other words, wear something that is comfortable and easy to try things on over, in case of long lines or even non-existent changing rooms. I like leggings, long slim-fitting tank or tee-shirt-style dresses, a loose-fitting cardigan and slip-on flats. If you are not wearing socks or knee highs, at least slip a pair in your purse for trying on shoes.

Many thrift stores run various specials, often offering discounts of anything with a different color tag every week. Another discount is anything dated over a month ago, and still another puts out a monthly calendar with different half-off items.

Know When To Clean It

Most of the clothes in thrift stores are clean. However, it is a good idea to invest in some dry cleaning for those second hand suits, pants, and coats. This will get rid of lingering smells that may not be pleasant.

Shop By Color

Most thrift stores organize their clothes by color and size.

SHOP BY PATTERN

If you like prints or floral patterns, they are generally grouped with their dominant colors on the racks, and that makes them easier to spot. Follow these tips and sooner or later you will turn up some hidden gem that your friends will ask you about.

SHOP BY FABRIC

Feel the difference between silk and silky-feeling materials. Anything that has to be dry cleaned should make you pause, since cleaning bills can negate bargain prices.

SHOP BY TYPE

Start with pants and jeans. Then move onto blouses, sweaters and jackets, followed by suits, shoes, boots, purses, etc.

CHAPTER 4

Seven Reasons to Be a Thrifter

REASON #1:

The economy is rough right now, but you can still create cute, affordable outfits with accessories for as little as $15.00. It may require digging a bit deeper, but you will realize you still found a good bargain.

REASON #2:

Thrifting is environmentally friendly. Instead of that item ending up in the dumpster, with a little bit of repair, accentuating, and recreating, you can offer suits, hats, dresses, handbags and jewelry another chance to prove their true worth.

REASON #3:

Usually thrift stores are run by non-profit organizations that donate the money to worthy causes, such as those living with HIV/AIDS, housing for the homeless and low income families.

REASON #4:

The 80s fashion era is back. You can find those big shoulder-padded boyfriend jackets, harem pants, neon-colored blouses, sparkling shirts, and tees, which have the musical DNA of 80s artists like Michael Jackson and Prince still vibrating in the threads of the clothing.

REASON #5:

Let's face it, not everyone is a size 4. If you are a size 12 and up, you can find tailored suits and dresses from other eras that are slimming and comfortable.

REASON #6:

Natural fabrics like linen, cotton, and silk are fine materials that were used in days gone by without so many synthetics mixed in. So if you're into the natural, there are finds out there waiting for you to take them home.

REASON #7:

The psychedelic 60s, disco 70s, and neon 80s clothing still hold some of the vibrancy and may even seem brighter due to certain dyes used back then.

CHAPTER 5

What's Color Got To Do With It?

Now let's talk about colors. Colors tell a lot about you. Did you know that black implies a sex appeal with a suggestion of sadness?

Red is provocative, and puts you in the mood for excitement, and is worn by the woman who wants to be exciting. Red is an extreme emotional color of fire and blood.

White is for purity, and white implies that you are good.

Yellow is for pleasure. A woman wearing yellow is likely to be a lively personality. A love for yellow shows a cool, clear brain.

Brown is for caution. A woman who often wears brown is probably a practical, dependable, conventional type that chooses brown because it means staying power.

Orange is for living. A woman in orange is most likely easy going. She likes good food and is a good socializer with a zest for the finer things in life.

Gray is for a woman who keeps her cool. She is self-assured. An elegant, conservative lady who looks sophisticated, but may be cool in other regards, too.

Lavender indicates a feeling of boredom. Here is the cautious, diplomatic type with quiet domestic tastes and conventional ideas; a look-before-you-leap kind of woman.

Blue is for the romantic. The woman who prefers lighter blues tends to be sincere, affectionate, and anxious to please.

The woman who chooses darker blues is likely to be somewhat more practical.

Purple is for power. It is the most difficult color to wear and is usually chosen by a power loving woman, a temperamental, who likes to express her feeling of superiority, especially to men.

Green is often worn by a worldly woman who is fed up with her complicated life. Tired or disillusioned, she wants to return to the simple life to a fresh rejuvenated lifestyle, and she may be hoping to find it through a man.

Baby Pink means security in love and men feel most comfortable with this color. If you are involved in a long relationship with a man, put on your pink. He'll probably prefer you in that color over any other.

If you follow these tips, you will become a Thrift Store Diva who looks like a runway super model stepping out of the pages of *Vogue* or *Essence* magazines, respectively.

CHAPTER 6

Let the Show Begin!!!!!!!!!

The following pages show some pictures of my outfits, how I have put them together, and also the prices I paid for them.

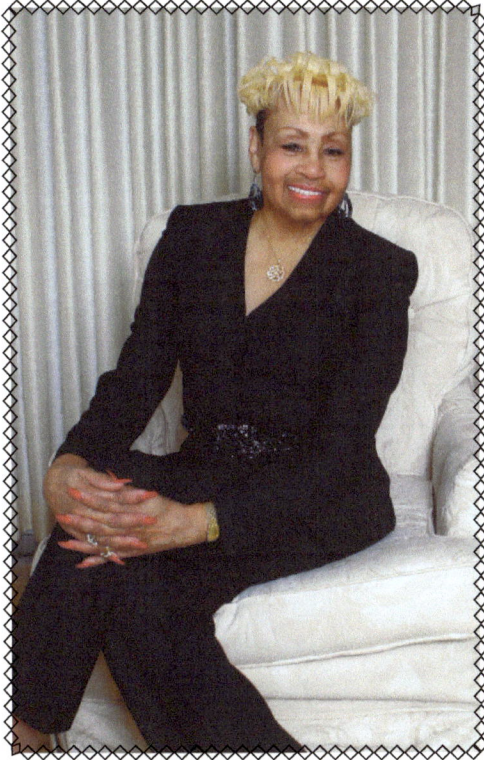

Black crepe pant suit with sequin beaded belt. It is designed by John Meyer. Purchased at Goodwill Thrift Store for $15.00. My black is beautiful.

You can spruce up your wardrobe without blowing your paycheck. Here's the proof.

Cover—wearing black wool jersey dress and coat ensemble with gold leather and fox fur inserts on dress and coat. Outfit purchased at Goodwill for $10.00. Outfit is accessorized with gold earrings and black leather boots. Cost of completed outfit is $25.00.

Gold skirt suit, puchased at Goodwill for $10.00

Turquoise dress, purchased at South Street thrift store for $4.99.

Emerald green skirt suit, purchased at AMVETS thrift store for $7.99.

St. John, black two-piece knit, with beaded collar, beads around bottom of sleeves and around the bottom of top, purchased at South Street thrift store for $15.00

St. John, bone knit dress, purchased at South Street thrift store for $15.00. Shoes purchased at Goodwill for $6.99.

Fox stole, purchased at Goodwill for $9.99.

Designer purses galore: Chanel, Dooney & Burke, none over $10.00.

More purses, all under $10.00, purchased at Salvation Army.

Jewelry purchased at South Street thrift store, all under $8.00 for each set. Be creative with your jewelry. Details do matter.

Furs and Animal Prints

Faux fur leopard vest: $7.99, hat: $3.99, purse: $3.99.
Faux fur brown mink vest: $7.99.
Fox collar: $2.99, fox hat: $9.99.
Faux fur gold jacket: $12.99, faux fur tiger purse, $4.99.

Brown pant suit with leather trim collar by Tahari, $10.00. Animal print blouse, $3.99. Mix and match pieces for intensity.

Bright coral pant suit, with colorful yellow and coral blouse. Don't shy away from adding color. Outfit purchased at Salvation Army, $13.00.

Black three-piece: long skirt, blouse and jacket, $9.00.

Black pant suit and white blouse—outfit, $10.00. My black is beautiful.

Bright lights and intense colors are in for spring. These suits are hot. Bright red, yellow and orange. Purchased at Salvation Army, $10.00 each. Also bright green, yellow, mauve suits purchased at Salvation Army, $10.00 each.

Peach suit, $5.99, purchased at Goodwill. Silver polka dot, $9.99, and mint green purchased at South Street thrift store, $7.99.

Beautiful colors of orange, fuscia, peach, green and rust are these bright and bold outfits from India, $5.99 each, purchased at Goodwill, Salvation Army, and South Street thirft stores.

A beautiful, bold orange and gold formal gown from India, $35.00. Shoes are gold beaded and sequin, $3.99.

These fierce prints are from Salvation Army, Goodwill, and AMVETS. The sequin dress, $5.99, the zebra suit, $10.00, zebra dress and sweater were $15.00. Rust pant suit, $10.00, and rust print blouse was $7.99.

Color brights are these bold colorful blouses—purchased for $5.49 each from Salvation Army.

Stepping out on the town in evening wear. White gown is brand new, $9.99.

Taupe gown, $9.99.

Multi-color gown, $7.99.

Shoes and more—gold sequin, gold slings, black slings, with gold and silver studs.

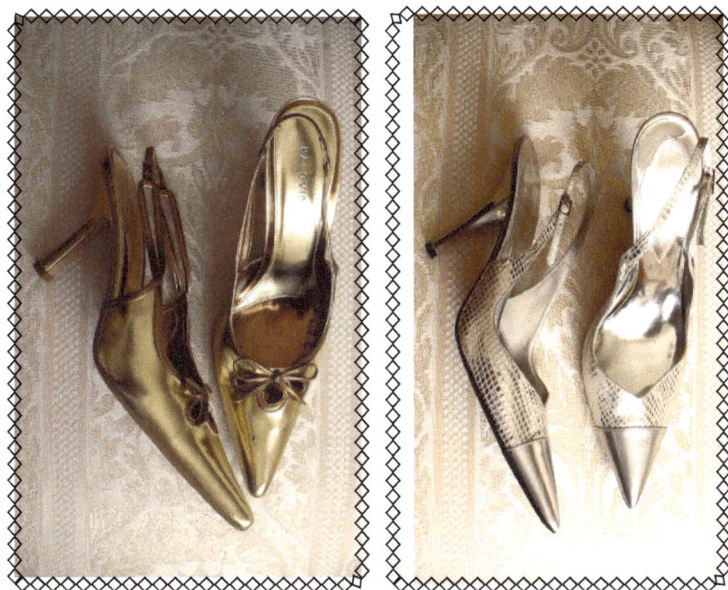

Gold slings, siliver slings, and bone pumps.

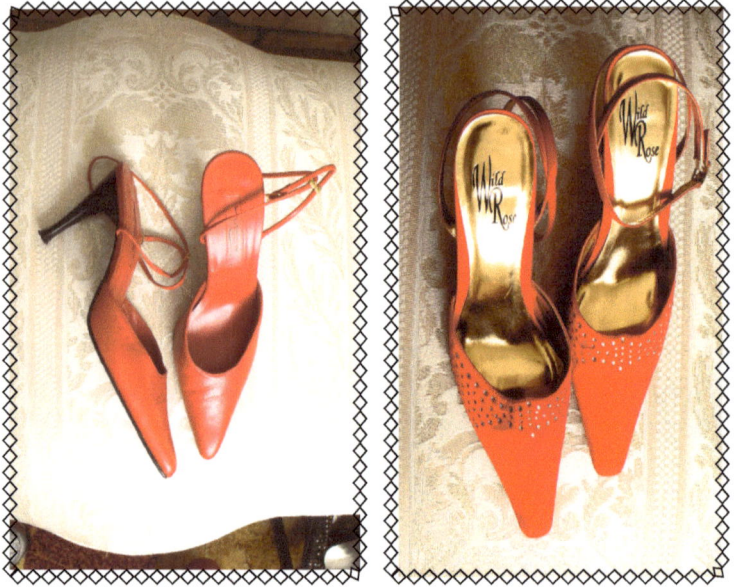

Red leather ankle straps, red pumps, and red crepe ankle
straps with rhinestones on the toe.

Multi-color sequin pumps, rose slings with polka dot
bows, and black satin pumps with beaded toe—each pair
was $6.99, purchased at Goodwill.

Bold, bright and beautiful, these outfits are popping and rocking.

If you have any flair for flare, you have to love this outfit. It's a show stopper.

This camel-hair cape is sporty, tailored and sleek. Purchased from South Street thrift store for $7.99.

The black wool cape is more formal and dressy, with beaded shoulders, and a stand-up collar. Purchased from Salvation Army for $10.99.

Louise and Helen, Best Friends Forever (BFF).

Doris Matthews, Helen Pearson's sister (Thrift Store Diva) is modeling two outfits that were purchased for her by Helen Pearson.

A black two-piece velvet evening gown with gold lace inserts on sleeves and down the front. This gown was purchased at Salvation Army for $8.99.

A Champaign Chiffon gown with matching stole that is out of the same lace fabric as the bodice of the gown. This gown was purchased at South Street Thrift Store for $7.99.

Conclusion

Let the clothes on the previous pages encourage women of all ages to be inspired to look their best, as their appearance glorifies God and honors Him. Christian women should be instruments of praise to God because we are watched, and our lives are scrutinized. How others interpret our appearance and actions, to a great extent, will be how they regard Christ and our example of having a Christ-like character.

Women dress themselves not merely to have outward adornment, but to use such adornment to emphasize what is within. Your outward adornment tells a lot about you. It is your image. It's what you portray before anyone knows you.

What I'm saying is, the way you walk, talk, carry yourself and dress gives a person some idea about what type of person you are. Therefore, we must make sure that the clothes we wear do not give an image that will dishonor God.

www.ingramcontent.com/pod-product-compliance
Lightning Source LLC
Chambersburg PA
CBHW041217270326
41931CB00001B/17